Preface

French for Kids 1 is a series of 3 course books. This is a first part for the earliest stage of learning French as a foreign language where students are not able to understand lots of rules of their maternal language. This book is useful in the primary schools of India and abroad. This is intended to help the beginners and parents as well to prepare their kids to start learning French as foreign language. This book provides a simple and interesting method of teaching to teachers and different ways of learning French to the students with an innovative and creative approach.

This book should be of value as this book is integrated with pictorial representations for better visual learning experience for the kids. In this book for the better understanding of our students every topic has different exercises for practice which can give confidence to the students.

At the end, I would like to say that the book is designed to equip both the teachers and the students with ideal guidance and exercises for practice.

Table of Contents

Lesson 1 (Leçon1): Alphabet (L'alphabet)

A aa		Aeroplane Avion
		Ass Âne
B bay		Ball Ballon
	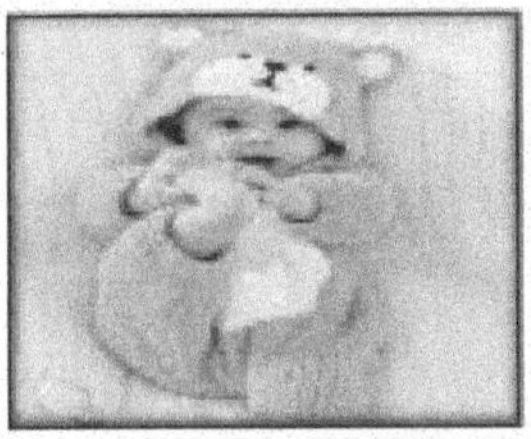	Baby Bébé

C say		Sky Ciel
		Cat Chat

D day		Dolphin Dauphin
		Flag Drapeau

E eh	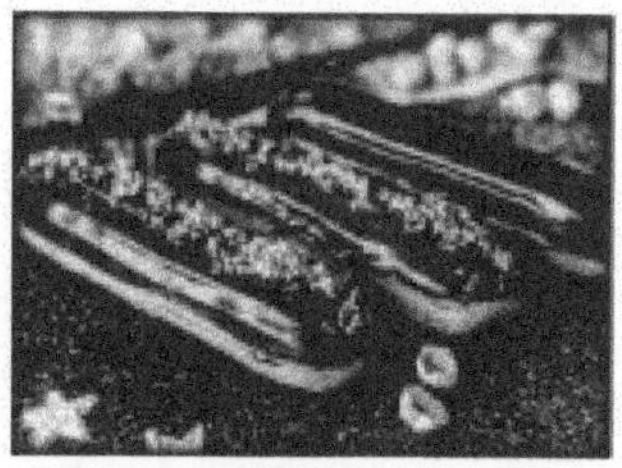	Eclairs Éclairs
		School École
F eff	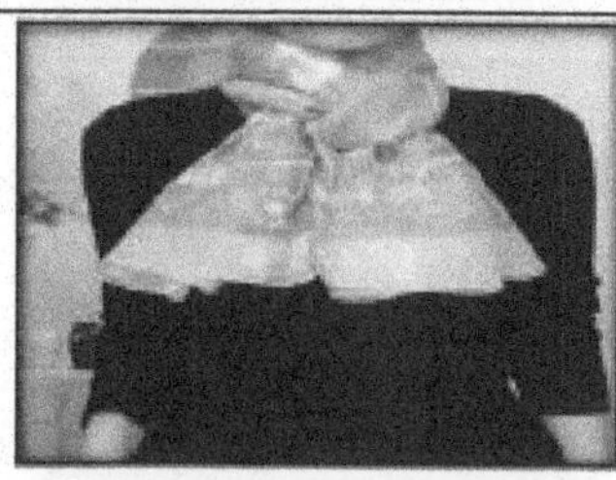	Muffler Foulard
		Fridge Frigo

G jay		Giraffe Girafe
		Eraser Gomme
H ash		Man Homme
		Owl Hibou

I ee		Image Image
		Igloo Igloo

J zhee		Toy Joujou
		Garden Jardin

K ka	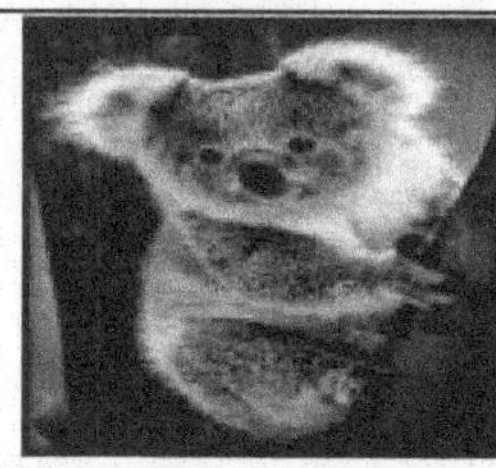	Koala Koala
		Kiwi Kiwi
L ell		Rabbit Lapin
		Moon Lune

M em		Honey Miel
		Mountain Montagne
N En		Night Nuit
		Teddy bear Nounours

O oo		Orange Orange
	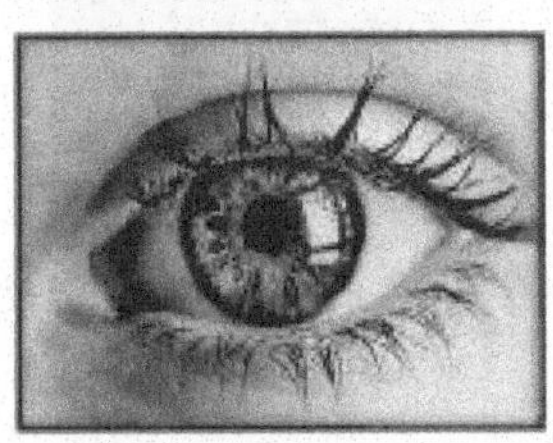	Eye

P Pay		Umbrella Parapluie
		Apple Pomme

Q kyu		Queue Queue
		Queue Queue
R err		King Roi
		Rose Rose

<table>
<tr><td rowspan="2">S
Ess</td><td></td><td>Sun
Soleil</td></tr>
<tr><td></td><td>Monkey
Singe</td></tr>
<tr><td rowspan="2">T
tay</td><td></td><td>Board
Tableau</td></tr>
<tr><td></td><td>Tag
Tag</td></tr>
</table>

<table>
<tr><td rowspan="2">U
Eu</td><td></td><td>Ukulele
Ukulélé</td></tr>
<tr><td></td><td>Unicorne
Unicorne</td></tr>
</table>

V vay		Car Voiture
		Suitcase Valise

W Dooble vay		Walkman Walkman
		Warrior Warrior
X iks		Squirral Xérus
	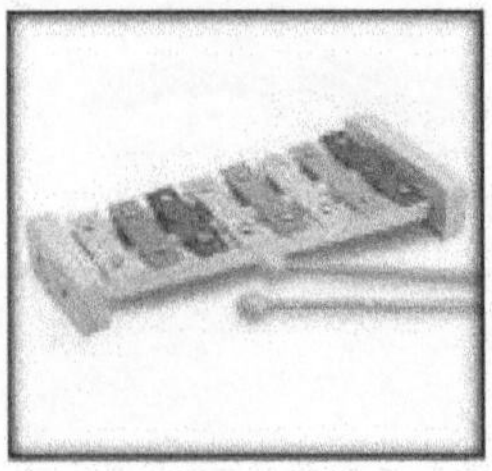	Xylophone Xylophone

Y igrek		Eyes Yeux
		Yo-yo Yo-yo
Z Zed		Zebra Zèbre
		Zoo Zoo

À Vous

Exercise 1: Tell the name with French pronounciation:

1	 VIEWLA	__VAY_EE_EH_DOOBLE-VAY_ ELL_ AA_
2	 SHUBH	________________________________
3	 CHANDNI	________________________________
4	 DIVYA	________________________________
5	 RIHIT	________________________________

Lesson 2 (Leçon2): I have eight candies. (J'ai huit bonbons.)

1	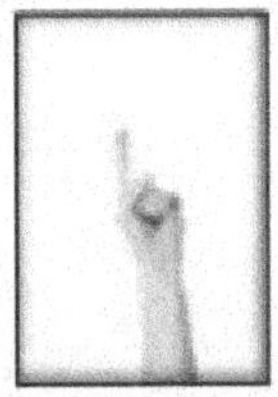	One Un
2	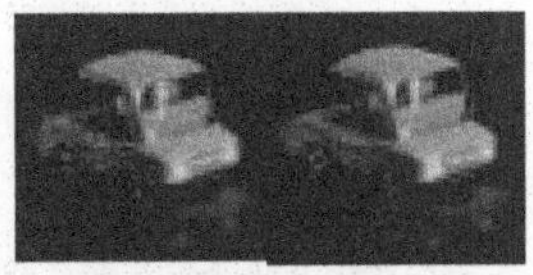	Two Deux
3	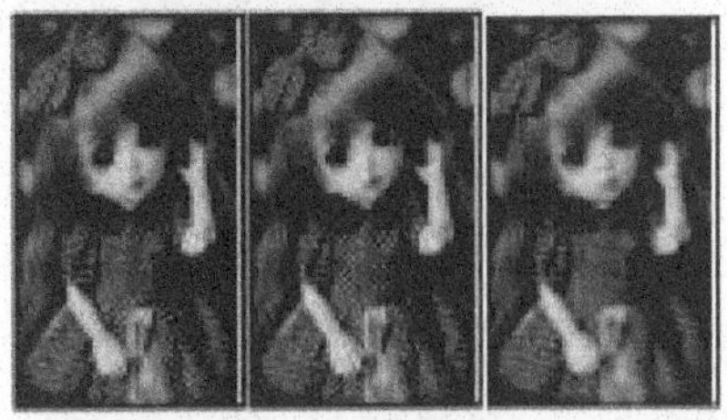	Three Trois
4		Four Quatre
5		Five Cinq

6		Six Six
7	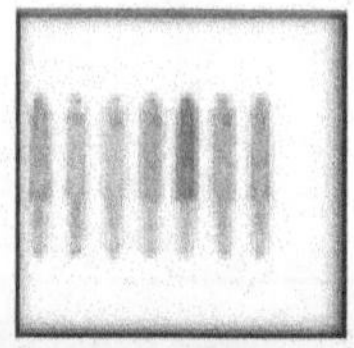	Seven Sept
8	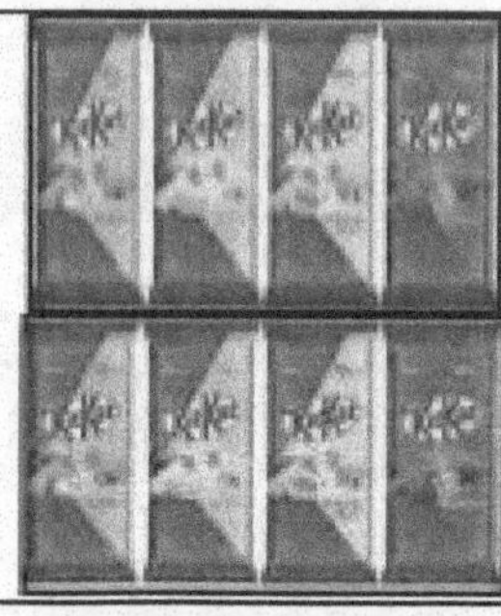	Eight Huit
9		Nine Neuf
10		Ten Dix

À Vous

Exercise 1: Count and match the following columns by drawing lines:

1		Quatre
2		Cinq
3		Trois
4		Deux
5		Un

Lesson 3 (Leçon3): Greet! everyone (Saluez! tout le monde)

Neha is coming to her Uncle's home. Without saying anything to uncle and aunty she run towards her cousins Chinmay and Tanvi.

Mother	:	Why you run inside? First you should greet your uncle and aunty then do whatever you want.
Neha	:	Ok Maman
Mother	:	Greet your uncle by "Bonjour"
Neha	:	Bonjour uncle !
Uncle	:	Bonjour ma chère!
Neha	:	Bonjour Aunty !
Aunty	:	Bonjour ma chère!

After greeting now Neha is playing with her cousins. Now her cousins are telling how she should greet according to timings.

Here are some greetings words which Neha can use in future:

Good morning	Bonjour	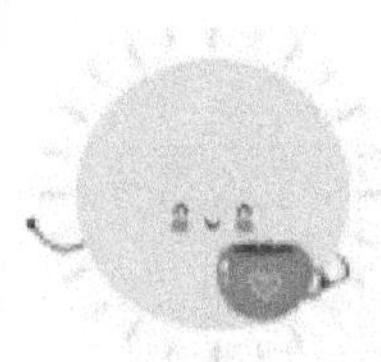
Good afternoon	Bon après-midi	

Good Evening	Bonsoir	
Good Night	Bonne nuit	

À Vous

Exercise 1: Now write greeting words by seeing images:

1. ________________

2. ________________

3. ________________

4. ________________

Lesson 4 (Leçon 4): I want to carry this to school (je veux porter ces choses à l'école)

Why it is so heavy, what is there in this bag???

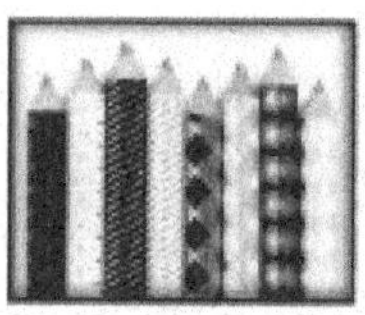	Pencil	Crayon
	Eraser	Gomme
	Sharpner	Taille-crayon
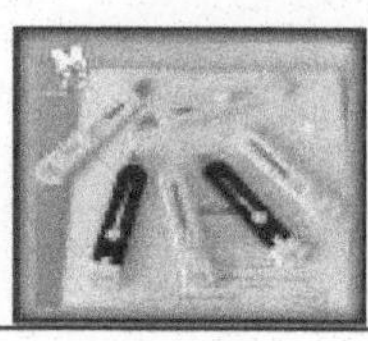	Paper cutter	Coupe-papier

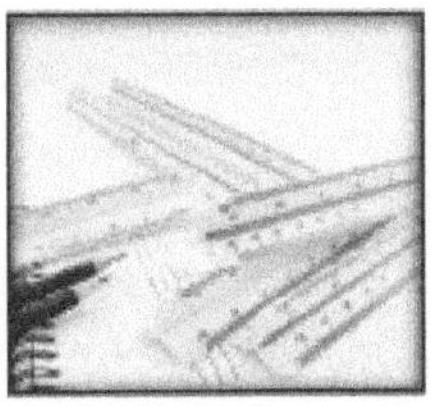	Scale	Rular
	Kit	trousse
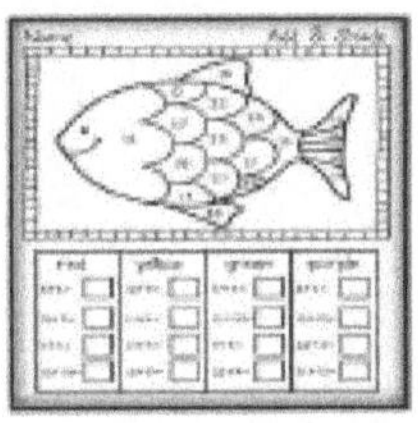	Worksheet	Feuille
	Bottle	Bouteille
	Lunch box	Boite du repas
	Books	Livres

	Note books	Cahiers

À Vous

Exercise 1: Tick the suitable things to keep in your bag.

1		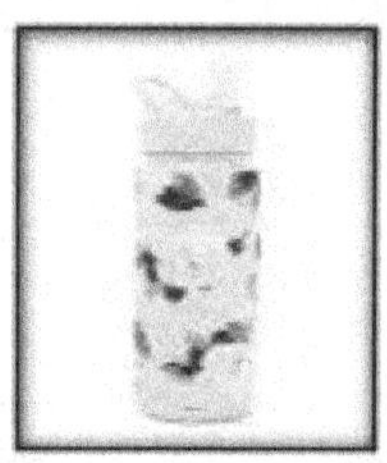		
2				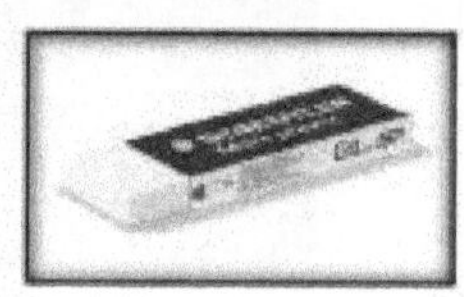
3				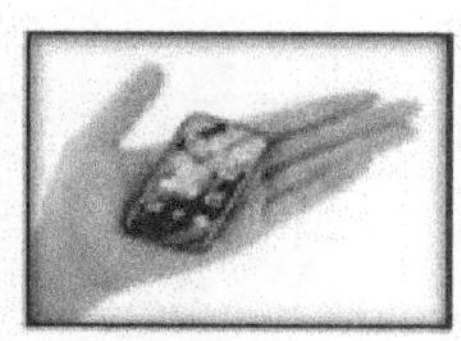

Lesson 5 (Leçon 5) : Food (La nourriture)

Fruits (Les fruits)		
	Apple	Pomme
	Mango	Mangue
	Orange	Orange
	Banana	Banane

	Grapes	Raison

Vegetables(Les Légumes)		
	Potato	Pomme de terre
	Tomato	Tomate
	Cauliflour	Choufleur
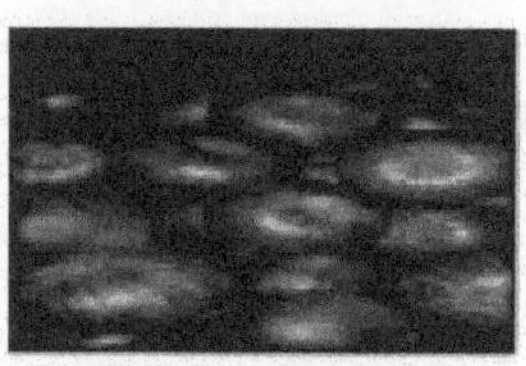	Onion	Oignon
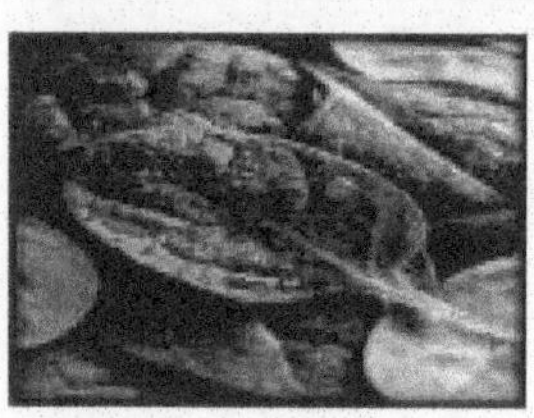	Spinach	Épinard

À Vous

Exercise 1: Draw one fruit and vegetable of your choice.

Lesson 6 (Leçon 6): Animals and birds (Les animaux et les oiseaux)

	Peacock	Paon
	Cock	Coq
	Elephant	Éléphant
	Chien	Dog

	Chat	Cat
	Lion	Lion
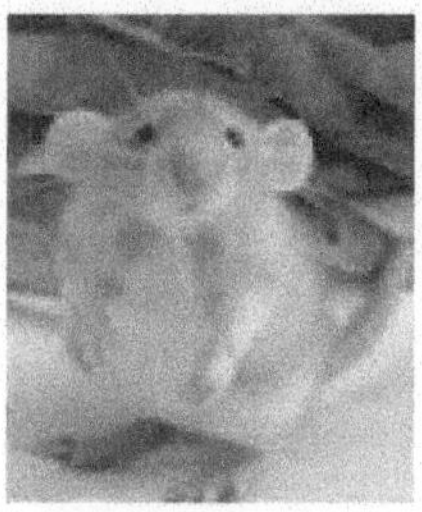	Rat	Rat

À Vous

Exercise 1 : Find out the animals and birds name from below grid.

R	A	T	N	V	F	D
N	D	N	M	S	C	H
T	A	A	J	D	E	J
Q	W	H	I	C	R	L
Z	E	P	A	O	N	I
W	R	É	P	Q	Y	Y
I	Y	L	I	O	N	R
P	O	É	B	C	H	B

Lesson 7 (Leçon7) : Colours of the world (Les couleurs du monde)

TIPPI TIPPI TOP

WHICH COLOUR YOU WANT

I Want

	Blue	Bleu
	Red	Rouge
	Yellow	Jaune
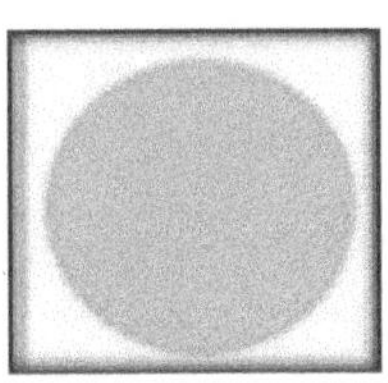	Orange	Orange

	Green	Vert
	Purple	Violet
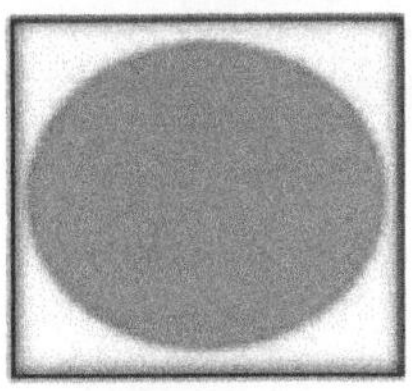	Pink	Rose
	Black	Noir
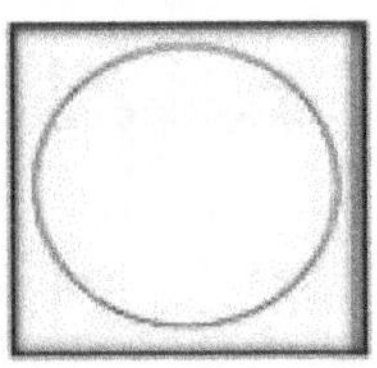	White	Blanc

À Vous

Exercise 1: Match the colour's name with correct coloured boxes:

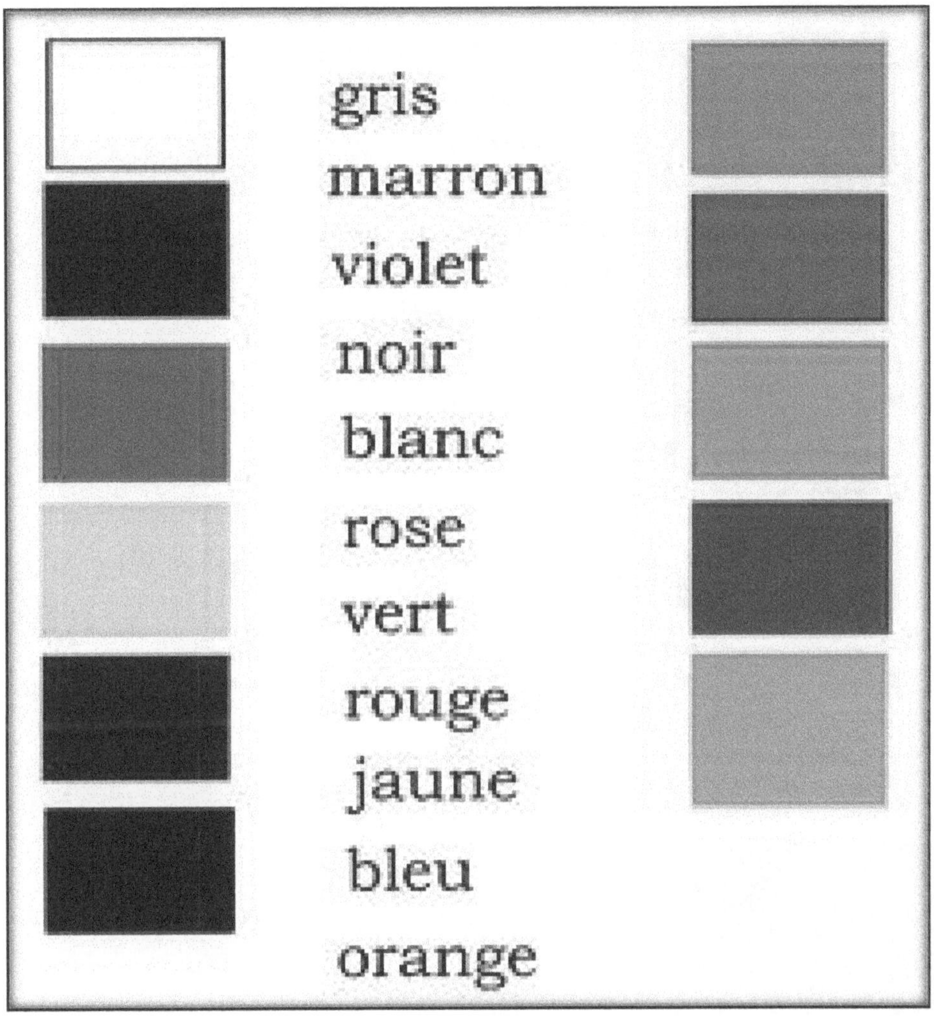

Lesson 8 (Leçon8): Parts of the body (Les parties du corps)

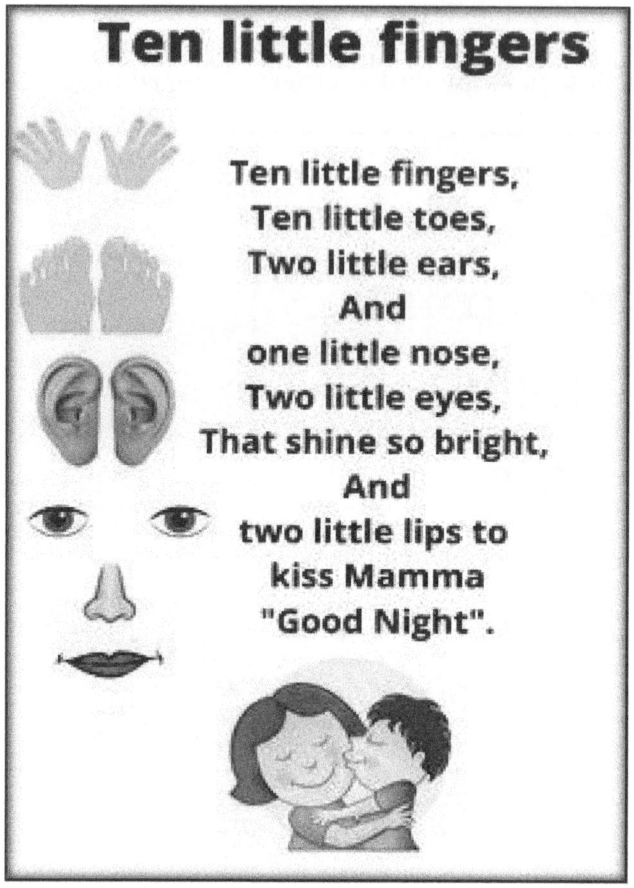

1	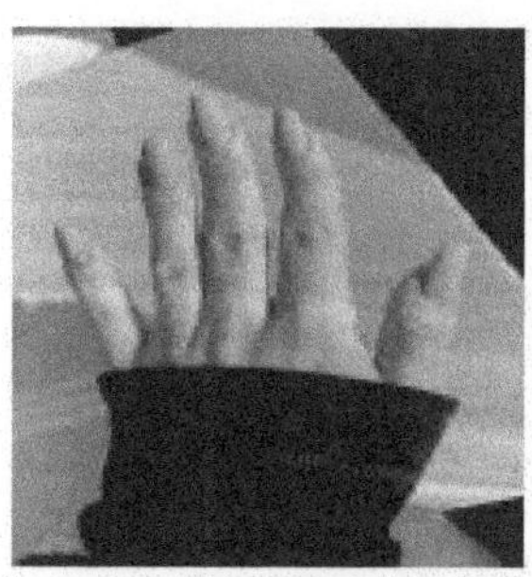	Fingers	Doigts
2	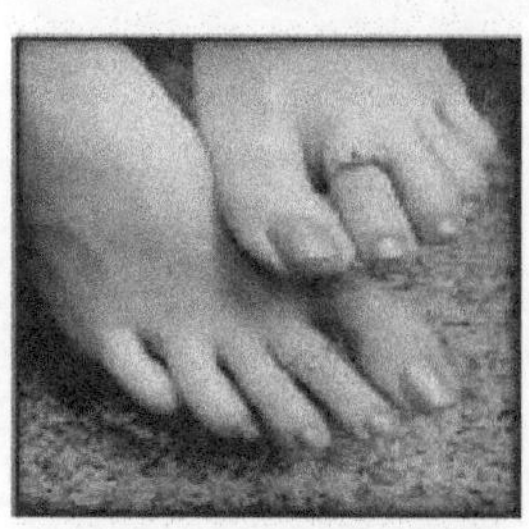	Toes	Orteils

3	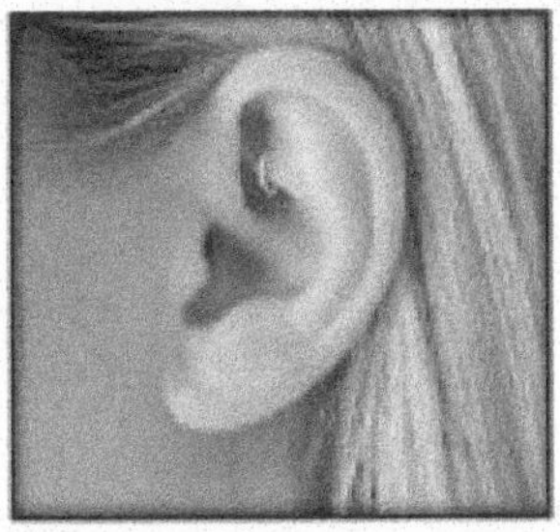	Ear	Oreille
4		Eyes	Yeux
5		Lips	Lèvres

À Vous

Exercise 1: Write the names of images.

1	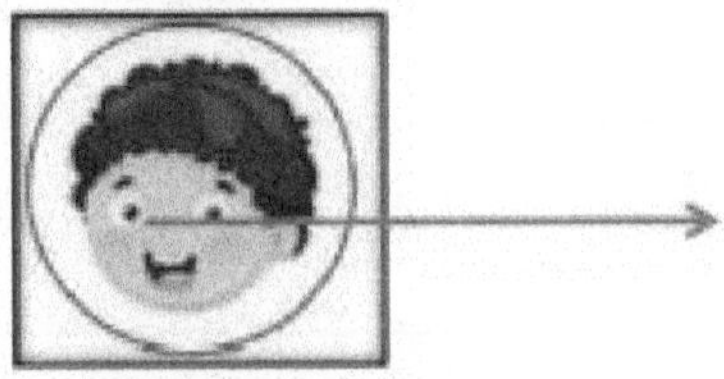	
2	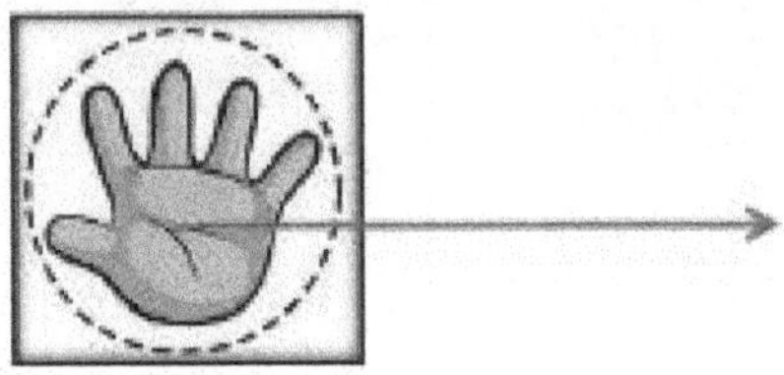	
3	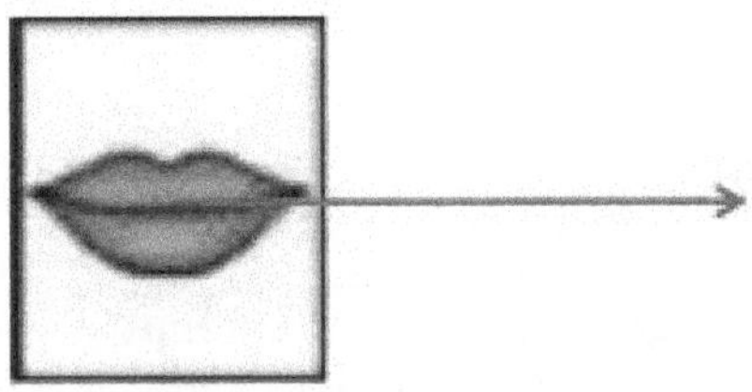	
4	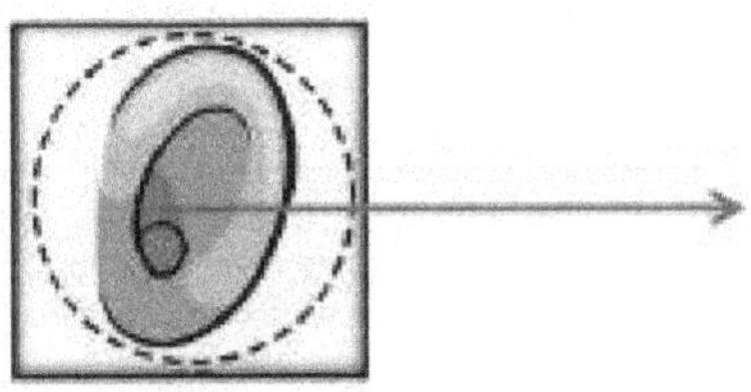	
5	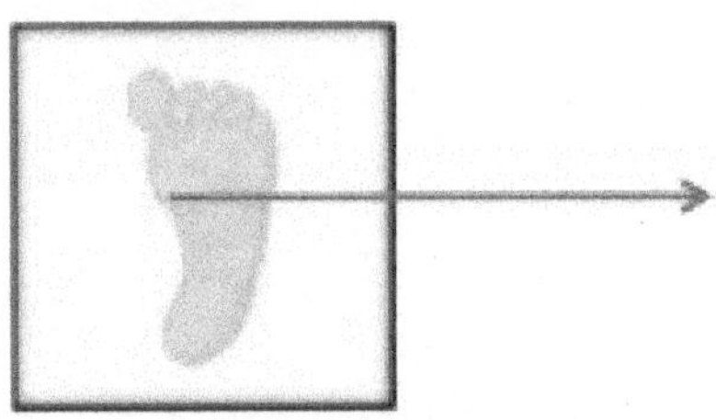	

À Vous

Answer key (Les réponses)

Leçon 1

Exercise 1:

1 Done for students
2 ESS ASH EU BAY ASH
3 SAY ASH AA EN DAY EN EE
4 DAY EE VAY IGREK AA
5 AIR EE ASH EE TAY

Leçon 2

Exercise 1:

1 Deux
2 Un
3 Quatre
4 Cinq
5 Trois

Leçon 3

Exercise 1:

1 BonneNuit
2 Bonjour
3 Bonsoir
4 Bon après midi

Leçon 4

Exercise 1:

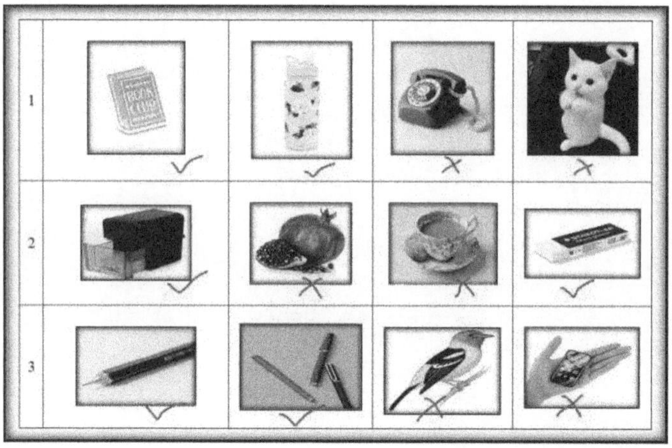

Leçon 5

Exercise 1: Draw as per your choice.

Leçon 6

Exercise 1:

R	A	T				
		N				
		A				
		H		C		
		P	A	O	N	
		É		Q		
		L	I	O	N	
		É				

Leçon 7

Exercise 1:

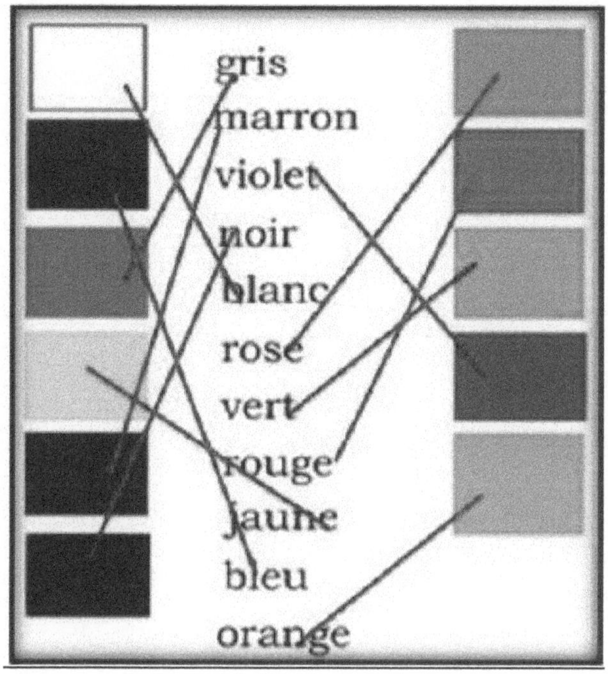

Leçon 8

Exercise 1:

1 Yeux
2 Main
3 Lèvres
4 Oreille
5 Pied

:   ;

Printed at Repro India Ltd.